Primary Sources of the Abolitionist Movement

John Brown and the Armed Resistance to Slavery

Rebecca Stefoff

Cavendish Square

New York

Published in 2016 by Cavendish Square Publishing, LLC
243 5th Avenue, Suite 136, New York, NY 10016

Copyright © 2016 by Cavendish Square Publishing, LLC

First Edition

Library of Congress Cataloging-in-Publication Data

Stefoff, Rebecca, 1951-
John Brown and armed resistance to slavery / Rebecca Stefoff.
pages cm. — (Primary sources of the abolitionist movement)
Includes bibliographical references and index.
ISBN 978-1-50260-534-4 (hardcover) ISBN 978-1-50260-535-1 (ebook)
1. Brown, John, 1800-1859—Juvenile literature. 2. Harpers Ferry (W. Va.)—History—John Brown's Raid, 1859—Juvenile literature. 3. Antislavery movements—United States—History—19th century—Juvenile literature.
4. Abolitionists—United States—Biography—Juvenile literature. I. Title.

E451.S848 2015
973.7116092—dc23
[B]

2015006165

Editorial Director: David McNamara
Editor: Amy Hayes
Copy Editor: Cynthia Roby
Art Director: Jeffrey Talbot
Senior Designer: Amy Greenan
Senior Production Manager: Jennifer Ryder-Talbot
Production Editor: Renni Johnson
Photo Researcher: J8 Media

CONTENTS

Before the Fire

John Brown was born at the dawn of the nineteenth century and died on the eve of the Civil War. He is seen today by some as a hero and **martyr**, by others as a **terrorist**. His story raises questions that are as important now as they were in his day: How far should a person go to support a cause? Is it ever right to commit acts of violence, even murder, for a goal believed to be noble and just?

Brown fought to end **slavery** in the United States. His fight was part of a larger national struggle, one that had been building since the early days of the American colonies.

In 1619, twenty African slaves were sold to colonists at Jamestown, Virginia, to work in the colony's tobacco fields. Many more followed. Historians estimate that 11.5 million Africans were carried by force to the Americas between the sixteenth and nineteenth centuries.

Although the majority went to the sugar plantations of South America and the Caribbean, every colony in North America had African slaves. They were most numerous in the South, where they toiled on tobacco farms, but enslaved Africans did much outdoor labor and household work in the North. Slavery in the United States took the form of **chattel slavery**, in which the law defines slaves as chattels, or property, with few or no rights.

During the eighteenth century a movement against slavery arose in Europe and North America. Some people opposed slavery on **moral** grounds, as a question of right and wrong. Not all of them believed that whites and blacks were equal, but they did believe it was wrong for one person to own another as property. They were outraged by the cruel and inhumane treatment suffered by many slaves.

Others opposed slavery for practical reasons. They argued that the work done by slaves should be done by free laborers. They also pointed to the history of violent uprisings by oppressed slaves. The thirteen North American colonies alone experienced more than 250 uprisings. Each was crushed, but each added to the fear that blacks would turn on whites. That happened in 1791 in the French colony of Saint-Domingue in the Caribbean. Slaves rebelled, burned plantations, killed whites, and even defeated a French army. The colony became the free black nation of Haiti in 1804.

Slavery also had a political dimension. In 1776, the English colonies of North America issued their stirring Declaration of Independence from Great Britain, saying:

"Am I not a man and a brother?" asks a British antislavery painting from the eighteenth century.

"We hold these truths to be self-evident, that all men are created equal." The newly created United States championed equality and liberty—but allowed slavery. This contradiction troubled some Americans.

Northern states began passing laws against slavery during the Revolutionary War. (Many laws took effect gradually, so that not all slaves were immediately freed.) In the South, however, cotton was increasingly important, and the ever-expanding fields of cotton plants demanded labor. Southern planters insisted that African slavery was essential to their survival.

By 1800, the year of John Brown's birth, the United States consisted of seventeen states: nine slave and eight free. Tension over the question of slavery was rising.

George Washington and Thomas Jefferson, the country's first and third presidents, were slave owners who worried that slavery might bring a crisis to the nation. Jefferson wrote that slavery, "like a fire bell in the night,

Taken around 1846 or 1847, this photograph is a primary source: the oldest-known image of John Brown.

awakened and filled [him] with terror." He was right to worry. Slavery would threaten the unity of the United States. John Brown's actions, some historians believe, were the spark that lit the roaring fire of the Civil War.

CHAPTER ONE

A Man with a Mission

J ohn Brown, who would one day be the most talked-about person in America, was born in Torrington, Connecticut, on May 9, 1800. His family had deep roots in national history. His father, Owen Brown, was descended from a man who had come to the Plymouth colony on the **Puritan** ship *Mayflower* in 1620. The ancestors of his mother, Ruth Mills Brown, had reached American shores soon afterward.

Owen Brown's father—John Brown's grandfather—died when Owen was five. The boy's mother was left struggling to care for her large family. When Owen grew up he became a tanner, a tradesperson who uses chemical treatment to turn rawhide into leather. In 1793, he married a minister's daughter and started his own family, which would eventually include eight children. The fourth was a son whom they named John.

Early Years

When John Brown was five, Owen Brown moved his family from Connecticut to the frontier of western Ohio. John's childhood was shaped by the hard work of a frontier life and by the stern religious faith in which he was raised. John's father had little patience for misbehavior. John was punished for wrongdoings, such as telling lies, by being whipped with a switch cut from a tree—a very common form of discipline at the time. He later declared that he was grateful for his strict and moral upbringing.

When Brown was in his early teens he had an experience that turned him against slavery. Years later, in 1859, he wrote about it in a letter to a teenager named Henry Stearns. In the letter Brown called himself "him" and "John," but he made it clear that he was writing about himself:

> During the war with England a circum-stance occurred that in the end made [John] a most *determined Abolitionist*: & led him to declare, *or Swear: Eternal war* with Slavery. He was staying for a short time with a very gentlemanly landlord ... who held a slave boy near his own age very active, inteligent and good feeling; & to whom John was under considerable obligation for numerous little acts of kindness. *The master* made a great pet of John: brought him to table with his first company; & friends; called their attention to every little smart thing he

Brown's birthplace in Torrington, Connecticut, appeared on a postcard in the early twentieth century.

said or did: ... while the *negro boy* (who was fully if not more than his equal) was badly clothed, poorly fed; *& lodged in cold weather*, & beaten before his eyes with Iron Shovels or any other thing that came first to hand. This brought John to reflect on the wretched, hopeless condition, of *Fatherless & Motherless slave children*: for such children have neither Fathers or Mothers to protect, & provide for them. He sometimes would raise the question *is God their Father?*

After Brown's death, an admirer named Franklin Benjamin Sanborn collected many writings by and about Brown and published them as *The Life and Letters of John Brown* in 1885. Although the collection was designed to show Brown in a heroic light, it is a valuable source of documents from his lifetime. By the time Brown wrote the letter to young Henry Stearns, he was already famous—or notorious—as an **abolitionist**. The letter showed that he had questioned slavery from an early age.

Like many frontier children, John Brown attended school for only a few weeks or months a year. He learned to read at home, however, and borrowed books from neighbors when he could. When John was sixteen, he and a younger brother went to Massachusetts to attend a school for religious studies. Because John had had less education than the other students, he fell behind. He tried another school in Connecticut, but he could not keep up there, either. The brothers returned to Ohio the following year.

Marriage, Family, and Business

John Brown became a tanner, like his father, but opened his own business. In 1820, he married Dianthe Lusk. Together they had seven children, although only five of them lived to adulthood. The Browns lived for a time in Pennsylvania before moving back to Ohio.

Dianthe Lusk Brown died in 1832. John was stricken with grief, but he had a household and a family of young children to care for. He soon married again, this time to sixteen-year-old Mary Ann Day. They would eventually have thirteen children. The risk of childhood death was a sad reality in the nineteenth century, and seven of Brown's second wife's children died young.

To support his growing family, Brown became involved in many business ventures. In addition to

David Walker's *Appeal*

A major document of the abolitionist movement was written and published by David Walker (1796–1830), a free black man born in North Carolina. Walker settled in Boston in 1825 and soon became one of the city's leading abolitionists.

In 1829, he published a booklet titled *Walker's Appeal*, addressed to the enslaved blacks of America. Walker reminded them that Haitian slaves had won freedom in battle. He urged his readers to battle slavery and racial prejudice. The destiny of the black people of the world, he claimed, lay in their own hands. In one controversial passage Walker wrote: "Now, I ask you, had you rather be killed than to be a slave to a tyrant, who takes the life of your mother, wife, and dear little children? … Believe this, that there is no more harm for you to kill a man, who is trying to kill you, than it is for you to take a drink of water when thirsty."

Southerners banned *Walker's Appeal*, terrified that it would spark a slave rebellion. Some Northern abolitionists praised Walker, while others felt that he had gone too far in approving of violence.

WALKER'S

APPEAL,

IN FOUR ARTICLES,

TOGETHER WITH

A PREAMBLE

TO THE

COLORED CITIZENS OF THE WORLD,

BUT IN PARTICULAR AND VERY EXPRESSLY TO THOSE OF THE

UNITED STATES OF AMERICA.

Written in Boston, in the State of Massachusetts, Sept. 28th, 1829.

Boston:
PRINTED FOR THE AUTHOR.

1829.

Mary Brown was photographed with two of her children. The date is unknown.

running the tannery, he raised cattle and sold leather. He invested in land in New York, where the Erie Canal was being built. Unfortunately, an economic crash caused Brown to lose everything. A court declared him bankrupt. Afterwards, he slowly gained skill as a breeder of sheep. In 1844, he and a partner went into business as wool dealers, but that business failed in 1849. The years that followed were a nonstop struggle with debt, poverty, lawsuits, and more business ventures.

At various times Brown's family lived in Pennsylvania, Ohio, and New York. In 1848 he settled Mary and his children on a farm in North Elba, New York. Brown, however, continued to spend much of his time in Massachusetts. There he not only dealt with business matters but also deepened his commitment to the antislavery movement.

The Abolitionist

The wool business had taken Brown to Boston and Springfield, Massachusetts, and from the mid-1840s he was frequently in those cities. He found Springfield to be a center for **abolitionism**, the movement to abolish, or end, slavery.

Brown already held strong antislavery views. In 1837, after an abolitionist and newspaper publisher named Elijah Lovejoy was killed by a proslavery mob in Illinois, Brown rose to his feet in the middle of a memorial service for Lovejoy and publicly dedicated himself to ending slavery. He asked every member of his family to do the same. Brown came to believe that God meant him to devote all his strength to the fight against slavery in the United States.

In Massachusetts, Brown spent time with abolitionist leaders, including African Americans Sojourner Truth and Frederick Douglass. He got to know white community leaders and businessmen who were abolitionists, including lawyer Wendell Phillips and journalist William Lloyd Garrison, who published the leading abolitionist newspaper, *The Liberator*. Brown helped the operations of the Underground Railroad, a network of antislavery activists and "safe houses" through which escaped slaves made their way to freedom.

Abolitionists were outraged in 1850 when the US Congress passed the Fugitive Slave Act. Since 1793, slaveholders had had the legal right to enter free states to reclaim escaped slaves, as long as they could prove ownership of the slaves before a judge. Many Northern states and communities, however, had passed laws preventing slaveholders from using their courts for such purposes. The 1850 Fugitive Slave Act overturned those laws. Now every court in the land—and every citizen—

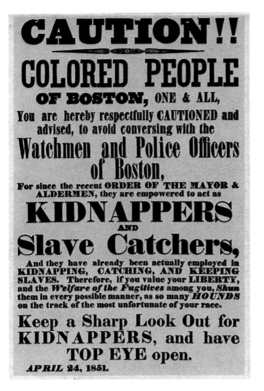

CAUTION!!

COLORED PEOPLE
OF BOSTON, ONE & ALL,

You are hereby respectfully CAUTIONED and advised, to avoid conversing with the

Watchmen and Police Officers of Boston,

For since the recent ORDER OF THE MAYOR & ALDERMEN, they are empowered to act as

KIDNAPPERS
AND
Slave Catchers,

And they have already been actually employed in KIDNAPPING, CATCHING, AND KEEPING SLAVES. Therefore, if you value your LIBERTY, and the *Welfare of the Fugitives* among you, *Shun* them in every possible manner, as so many *HOUNDS* on the track of the most unfortunate of your race.

Keep a Sharp Look Out for KIDNAPPERS, and have TOP EYE open.

APRIL 24, 1851.

Black Bostonians in 1851 are warned to beware of slavers and kidnappers

was required to help slaveholders recover their "property." Bands of slave catchers swarmed into Northern states, seizing black people, many of whom were free men and women, not escaped slaves, and taking them South.

Brown reacted to the passing of the Fugitive Slave Act by organizing forty-four free black men and women into a self-defense group in Springfield. Many such groups were formed by both black and by white abolitionists. Their purpose was to help blacks protect themselves against slave catchers. Some methods included giving warnings, pouring boiling water on would-be kidnappers, or rescuing other black people who had been seized by the slave catchers.

Brown called his group the League of Gileadites. He wrote down the following advice for its members:

> *No jury can be found in the Northern States*
> *that would convict a man for defending*
> *his rights to the last extremity. This is well*

understood by Southern Congressmen, who insisted that the right of trial by jury should not be granted to the fugitive ...

Should one of your number be arrested, you must collect together as quickly as possible, so as to outnumber your adversaries who are taking an active part against you. Let no able-bodied man appear on the ground unequipped, or with his weapons exposed to view: let that be understood beforehand. Your plans must be known only to yourself, and with the understanding that all traitors must die, wherever caught and proven to be guilty ... Do not delay one moment after you are ready: you will lose all your resolution if you do. Let the first blow be the signal for all to engage; and when engaged do not do your work by halves, but make clean work with your enemies, and be sure you meddle not with any others. By going about your business quietly, you will get the job disposed of before the number that an uproar would bring together can collect; and you will have the advantage of those who come out against you, for they will be wholly unprepared with either equipments or matured plans; all with them will be confusion and terror. Your enemies will be slow to attack you after you have done up the work nicely ...

Be firm, determined, and cool; but let it be understood that you are not to be driven to desperation without making it an awful dear job to others as well as to you … That would be taking them at their own words. You may make a tumult in the court-room where a trial is going on, by burning gunpowder freely in paper packages, if you cannot think of any better way to create a momentary alarm, and might possibly give one or more of your enemies a hoist. But in such case the prisoner will need to take the hint at once, and bestir himself; and so should his friends improve the opportunity for a general rush. A lasso might possibly be applied to a slave-catcher for once with good effect. Hold on to your weapons, and never be persuaded to leave them, part with them, or have them far away from you.

Stand by one another and by your friends, while a drop of blood remains; and be hanged, if you must, but tell no tales out of school. Make no confession.

Brown did not lead the League of Gileadites in action, but his words show that he thought slavery's enemies must take up arms to fight for their cause, even if it meant defying the law. Soon he would put that belief into action.

From "Bleeding Kansas" to Harpers Ferry

The United States suffered many growing pains in the nineteenth century. As new states were added to the Union, the **federal** government struggled to balance the number of slave and free states. In 1820, a deal called the Missouri Compromise had let Missouri enter the Union as a slave state while banning slavery throughout most of the western territories.

The deal collapsed in 1854, when Congress passed the Kansas-Nebraska Act. Kansas and Nebraska were getting close to statehood, and the new law said that settlers

Ten years after the photograph on page 7, this 1856 portrait reveals a careworn John Brown.

in the territories could choose for themselves whether to allow slavery. Nebraska was sure to be a free state, but Kansas was up for grabs.

Southerners were determined to make Kansas a slave state. Northerners were determined to fill it with "Free-Soilers" who would vote against slavery. Missouri sent groups of armed thugs called Border Ruffians into Kansas to terrorize antislavery settlers. Abolitionists in the East raised money to send rifles to the antislavery settlers in Kansas. The stage was set for battle, and John Brown would be in the thick of it.

"The Old Terrifier"

Five of Brown's adult sons moved to Kansas with their families, settling near the Free-Stater town of Lawrence. Soon afterward, in early 1855, John Jr. wrote to their father, asking him to come soon and to bring guns. The letter convinced Brown to devote himself full time to the fight against slavery, starting in Kansas. He headed west with his sixteen-year-old son Oliver and his daughter

FORCING SLAVERY DOWN THE THROAT OF A FREESOILER

An antislavery cartoon from around 1856 highlights the conflict in "Bleeding Kansas." Brown contributed to the violence there.

Ruth's husband. After they reached the Brown brothers' settlement, "Old Brown," as people soon started calling him, built a log cabin and organized a local defense force. Brown wanted to attack a Ruffian camp, but the townspeople chose not to strike the first blow.

In May 1856, Ruffians attacked Lawrence and destroyed much of the town. Several days later, Brown led five of his sons and a few other men in a raid on cabins known to house proslavery settlers. They dragged five men from their homes. Brown shot one. The others were slain with swords. None of the victims owned slaves. None had attacked Lawrence. Brown chose them for death in order to terrorize proslavery settlers.

Afterward Brown lied, saying he had not done any of the killing, but many people knew the truth. Proslavery settlers called Brown "the old terrifier." Violence and

The Secret Six

John Brown received aid from abolitionists who supported his actions. His most dedicated supporters, called the Secret Six, were Gerrit Smith, a politician and activist who had sold Brown the North Elba farm; Franklin B. Sanborn, a teacher; Theodore Parker, a minister; Samuel Gridley Howe, a doctor; George Luther Stearns, a businessman; and Thomas Wentworth Higginson, a minister who, in 1854, led armed abolitionists to rescue a captured slave in Boston. This rescue resulted in the death of a law enforcement officer.

In 1857, some of these men gave Brown money and rifles that he said would be used in Kansas, although he intended to use them in Virginia. Later he told the Secret Six that he would raid Virginia and launch a slave uprising, but not where the raid would take place. Several feared that Brown was doomed, but they agreed with Smith, who said, "Our dear friend has made up his mind to this course, and cannot be turned from it. We cannot give him up to die alone; we must support him." Their money paid for Brown's raid, including the weapons he carried into Virginia.

loathing between proslavery and antislavery groups spun out of control. Armed bands on both sides prowled the countryside. Brown took part in several actions, including a courageous fight against a much larger force of Ruffians at Osawatomie, near the Brown settlement, where Brown's son Frederick was killed.

Northern newspapers dubbed the troubled territory "Bleeding Kansas." The fight over slavery there claimed fifty-six lives before a new governor and the US Calvary

This drawing of the 1856 proslavery attack on Lawrence, Kansas, was published seven years later, in the middle of the Civil War.

ended the violence, not long after the Battle of Osawatomie. In the fall of 1856, Brown and his sons left Kansas, which would enter the Union as a free state in 1861. Brown already had another goal in view.

Into Virginia

In 1857, Brown spoke to abolitionist groups in Connecticut and Massachusetts, talking about his experiences in Kansas and raising money for the cause. In Connecticut he arranged to have made a thousand iron pikes, six-foot spears with knife-like blades attached. A man named H. N. Rust, who helped with this plan, described his time with Brown in a letter:

> During one of [Brown's] visits I carried him to Canton to see his relatives. Not far from their house he noticed a tombstone leaning against the stone wall by the roadside. He got out and examined it, and found it

to be his grandfather's; whereupon he said, "I will go back and see if my cousins will let me have it." They consented, and afterwards brought it to me at Collinsville; and I sent it to his address at North Elba. "That stone," said he, "formerly marked the grave of my grandfather, who died fighting for the liberties of his country; my son has just been murdered in the same cause in Kansas, and the Government applauded the murderer. This stone shall bear his name also; and I will have it set up at North Elba."

In the two years that followed, Brown moved between Massachusetts and Kansas, sometimes using an alias and wearing a long beard to hide his identity. He raised money and found followers, secured weapons and military training for his followers, and discussed his plans with Frederick Douglass and others. Several times he went to Canada, once leading to freedom some former slaves he had liberated during a raid into Missouri. All the while he was quietly planning an invasion into slaveholding land: Virginia. He had come to believe that only by striking a blow at the heart of slavery could he accomplish his mission.

Brown's target was Harpers Ferry, a town on a stretch of flat land between the Potomac and Shenandoah rivers. (Today Harpers Ferry is in

One of the thousand iron pikes that Brown shipped to Harpers Ferry. He planned to arm rebellious slaves with them.

West Virginia, which split off from Virginia to become a separate state in 1863.) It was the site of a federal **arsenal** where the government stored a large quantity of firearms and ammunition. Brown thought that by seizing the arsenal he could obtain weapons for the people who would flock to follow him, both free people and rebellious slaves.

In July 1859, under the name Isaac Smith, Brown rented a Maryland farmhouse close to Harpers Ferry. He had his stockpile of rifles and pikes shipped to the house in boxes labeled "Tools," and he sent word for his followers to join him. Only twenty-one came, fewer than he had expected. Mary Brown, feeling that the venture was dangerous, refused to join her husband, but Brown's teenage daughter and daughter-in-law served as cooks and lookouts.

Brown's followers believed they were there to make a quick raid on slaveholders and free their slaves. He did not tell them about the arsenal until shortly before the attack. He did confide the details of his plan to Frederick Douglass in a secret meeting in Pennsylvania. Brown wanted Douglass to join him. Douglass later described their conversation in *The Life and Times of Frederick Douglass* (1881):

> The taking of Harper's Ferry, of which Captain Brown had merely hinted before, was now declared as his settled purpose, and he wanted to know what I thought of it. I at once opposed the measure with all the arguments at my command. To me such a

Abolitionist Frederick Douglass tried in vain to talk his friend Brown out of attacking Harpers Ferry.

measure would be fatal to running off slaves (as was the original plan), and fatal to all engaged in doing so. It would be an attack upon the Federal government, and would array the whole country against us.

Captain Brown did most of the talking on the other side of the question. He did not at all object to rousing the nation; it seemed to him that something startling was just what the nation needed. He had completely renounced his old plan, and thought that the capture of Harper's Ferry would serve as notice to the slaves that their friends had come, and as a trumpet to rally them to his standard. He described the place as to its means of defense, and how impossible it would be to dislodge him if once in possession.

Of course I was no match for him in such matters, but I told him, and these were my words, that all his arguments, and all his descriptions of the place, convinced me that he was going into a perfect steel-trap, and that once in he would never get out alive;

that he would be surrounded at once and escape would be impossible. He was not to be shaken by anything I could say, but treated my views respectfully, replying that even if surrounded he would find means for cutting his way out; but that would not be forced upon him; he should, at the start, have a number of the best citizens of the neighborhood as his prisoners and that holding them as hostages he should be able, if worse came to worse, to dictate terms of egress from the town.

I looked at him with some astonishment … Our talk was long and earnest; we spent the most of Saturday and a part of Sunday in this debate—Brown for Harper's Ferry, and I against it; he for striking a blow which should instantly rouse the country, and I for the policy of gradually … drawing off the slaves to the mountains, as at first suggested and proposed by him.

Unable to change his friend's mind, Douglass left, fearing that what Brown was about to do might "rivet the fetters more firmly than ever on the limbs of the enslaved."

The Raid on Harpers Ferry

The raid began on the night of October 16, 1859. Brown and some of his men broke into the US Armory grounds, taking the watchman hostage. Brown sent several men

An 1864 map of Harpers Ferry shows the heights and hills from which townsfolk fired down on Brown and his men.

to the arsenal and several to the rifleworks, where guns were made.

Other members of the group had captured three white citizens and their slaves and brought them to the armory. Only one slave took the pike Brown offered and sided with the raiders—a sign that perhaps the local slaves would not rally behind Brown as he had expected. Next, Brown made a big mistake in letting a train leave Harpers Ferry. He had cut the local telegraph wires, but only eighteen miles away was another train station with a working telegraph. Soon the federal government knew what was happening in Harpers Ferry.

Citizens of the town and countryside, meanwhile, had armed themselves and surrounded the armory, firing down from the hills on the raiders. Three of Brown's men were pinned down in the rifle works. Brown, other followers, and the hostages were trapped in the engine

HARPER'S FERRY INSURRECTION—INTERIOR OF THE ENGINE-HOUSE, JUST BEFORE THE GATE IS BROKEN DOWN BY THE STORMING PARTY—COL. WASHINGTON AND HIS ASSOCIATES AS CAPTIVES, HELD BY BROWN AS HOSTAGES.

An artist's idea, based on witness statements, of Brown and the rebels just before troops broke down the door and captured them.

house with no food or water. Fighting raged through the following day, with injuries and deaths on both sides as townspeople repeatedly attacked the engine house.

On October 18, a train brought a hundred US Marines to Harpers Ferry. Their commander was Robert E. Lee, who later would be the leading Southern general in the coming Civil War. Lee offered the raiders a chance to surrender. Brown refused. The Marines smashed the engine-house door and, in three minutes, had killed or captured the raiders. Brown was wounded by a sword and knocked unconscious.

Ten of Brown's men, including two of his sons, were killed in the raid. Four townspeople and one Marine were also killed. No hostages were harmed. Eleven raiders escaped—six were later captured. One of the five who were never captured was Brown's son Owen. The slaves Brown had hoped to free were returned to their owners.

CHAPTER THREE

On Trial

J ohn Brown and those captured with him were imprisoned in the jail at Charles Town, about eight miles from Harpers Ferry. They would stand trial at the courthouse across the street.

The Virginia authorities underestimated the interest that the press and the public would take in Brown's trial. Reporters came to Charles Town from all over, and from his cell Brown carried what amounted to a public relations campaign. His letters, statements in court, and interviews with journalists were all designed to draw sympathy to his cause.

Charges and Claims

On October 25, Brown was charged with three crimes: murder, **treason** against Virginia, and **conspiracy** to **incite** a slave rebellion. All three charges carried the death penalty. Brown's trial began almost immediately.

In the meantime, Lee's troops had found Brown's storehouse of weapons, as well as some documents hidden in his headquarters, which included letters from his backers, the Secret Six. These were soon leaked to the newspapers, raising Southern outrage to new heights. Brown and his followers had had the support of leading citizens of the North!

The *Federal Union* of Milledgeville, Georgia, was among the Southern newspapers that declared the Harpers Ferry raid to be part of an organized attack on the South. It also declared that if the abolition movement was not "put down," the result could be "civil war":

> In our columns this week will be found further particulars concerning the **insurrection** at Harper's Ferry. There can no longer be any doubt but what this was a regularly concocted, and premeditated attempt of Abolition Fanatics to overthrow the Government, and emancipate the slaves … Without such positive proof, it would

be difficult to believe that such fools could be found running at large in the United States … Will not honest and conscientious men at the north now see the necessity of putting down a party whose principles, if carried out, can lead only to civil war, murder, and rapine?

As for the Secret Six, most of them panicked. Several fled the country for fear they would be arrested. Not one ever was, although the reason for this is unknown. Frederick Douglass, afraid that his knowledge of Brown's plan might result in his arrest, also went to England for two years.

The courthouse where Brown was tried still stands today. It was packed during his sensational trial.

The Trial

Claiming illness, Brown refused to stand up for most of his trial. Drawings published in the newspapers of the time show him lying on a cot. Some people were sympathetic to the sick, old man. Others called Brown a liar and coward.

Northern abolitionists paid lawyers to defend Brown. One of the lawyers' tactics backfired, spectacularly. They hoped to show that Brown was insane and therefore could not be held responsible for his actions—that he should be in an **asylum**, not

Brown spent most of his trial lying on a cot. Some people were sympathetic to him, but others were scornful.

facing the death penalty. One piece of evidence was a letter from Brown's half-brother Jeremiah, that read: "From his manner and his conversation … I had no doubt [John Brown] had become insane on the subject of slavery."

Hearing Jeremiah's letter read in court, Brown jumped up from his cot and angrily called the letter an insult. "I am perfectly unconscious of insanity, and I reject, so far as I am capable, any attempt to interfere in my behalf on that score," he declared. His legal team dropped that tactic.

Across the country there were three general opinions about Brown's sanity. Many Southerners, eager to see him executed, considered the insanity defense a cowardly trick. Many Northerners who were not abolitionists wanted him to be judged insane and committed to an asylum, and some Southerners agreed. This would remove Brown from the headlines and prevent him from becoming a martyr. Abolitionists, however, furiously denied Brown's insanity. They did not want his fight against slavery to look like the result of a diseased mind. In addition, they hoped that execution would make him a martyr, rallying people to the cause. "Let no one pray that Brown be spared," wrote abolitionist and minister Henry Ward Beecher. "Let Virginia make him a martyr … [A]nd round up Brown's failure with a heroic success." Brown shared this view. More than once he said that God intended for him to be captured, and that his execution would do more for abolitionism than he had done in life.

On October 31, the jury brought a verdict of guilty on all charges. (The other captured raiders, tried after Brown, were also found guilty.) Before Brown's sentence was pronounced, the judge invited him to speak. Brown delivered a speech that was soon reprinted thousands of times, as he knew it would be:

> I have, may it please the court, a few words to say. In the first place, I deny everything but what I have all along admitted—the design on my part to free the slaves. I intended certainly to have made a clean thing of that matter … That was all I intended. I never did intend murder, or treason, or the destruction of property, or to excite or incite slaves to rebellion, or to make insurrection … This court acknowledges, as I suppose, the validity of the law of God. I see a book kissed here which I suppose to be the Bible, or at least the New Testament. That teaches me that all

things whatsoever I would that men should do to me, I should do even so to them. It teaches me, further, to "remember them that are in bonds, as bound with them." I endeavored to act up to that instruction ... I believe that to have interfered as I have done—as I have always freely admitted I have done—in behalf of His despised poor was not wrong, but right. Now, if it is deemed necessary that I should forfeit my life for the furtherance of the ends of justice, and mingle my blood further with the blood of my children and with the blood of millions in this slave country whose rights are disregarded by wicked, cruel, and unjust enactments—I submit; so let it be done! ... I feel no consciousness of guilt. I have stated that from the first what was my intention and what was not. I never had any design against the life of any person, nor any disposition to commit treason, or excite slaves to rebel, or make any general insurrection. I never encouraged any man to do so, but always discouraged any idea of that kind.

Brown's claim that slavery was unjust and that he had tried only to act on God's instructions was powerful and heartfelt. Yet, there is no getting around the fact that Brown lied in this speech, as he had done several times during his trial. He denied ever having planned to incite, or even thinking about, an insurrection. This was untrue, as shown by the stockpile of weapons he had brought for arming slaves and by his statements to Douglass and others that he intended to start a mass uprising among Southern blacks.

Death Sentence

Brown was sentenced to death. He would be hanged on December 2, 1859. The other raiders also received the death penalty.

During the month between his sentencing and his execution, journalists and **orators** across the land continued to talk about Brown and the Harpers Ferry raid. On November 19, for example, *Harper's Weekly* published a front page with drawings of Southern blacks wielding knives and pikes, as if Brown inspired the slaves to take up arms. But the drawings were meant as **satire**, to make Brown's raid and the idea of a slave revolt appear ridiculous.

Harper's Weekly used satirical cartoons to mock Brown's failed attempt to start a slave rebellion.

Most responses were serious. Henry David Thoreau, abolitionist and the author of *Walden* (1854), made a speech in which

French author Victor Hugo, shown here three years after Brown's death, called Brown an "angel of light."

he called Brown an "angel of light." Victor Hugo, a French author who had left his country as a political exile, wrote a letter that appeared in newspapers in the United States and Europe. In it, Hugo said: "Politically speaking, the murder of John Brown would be an uncorrectable sin. It would create in the Union a latent fissure that would in the long run destroy it … Morally speaking, it seems a part of the human light would put itself out, that the very notion of justice and injustice would hide itself in darkness."

Hugo was not the only one to fear that Brown might cause a fissure, or split, in the Union that bound the states together. The free and slave parts of the United States had long been on the brink of open conflict. Although no single person can be blamed for starting a conflict as huge and long lasting as the Civil War, many modern historians agree that Brown played a key part in tipping the balance toward war.

Brown received a steady stream of visitors during November. Many of them told the reporters who clustered outside the jail how calm, kind, dignified, and inspiring the old man had been during their visits. Brown did not want Mary to visit him, however. He felt that it would cause them both pain. On November 8 he wrote to Mary and his children to say farewell and that his death would help the abolitionist movement:

Dear Wife & Children *Every One*

I will begin by saying that I have in some degree recovered from my wounds; but that I am yet quite weak in my back & sore about my left kidney. My appetite has been quite good for most of the time since I was hurt. I am supplied with almost every thing I could desire to make me comfortable, and the little that I do lack (some few articles of clothing which I lost) I may perhaps soon get again. I am besides quite cheerful having (as I trust) the peace of God which passeth all understanding to "rule in my heart" and the testimony (in some degree) of a good conscience that I have not lived altogether in vain. I can trust God with both the time and the manner of my death; believing as I now do that for me at this time to seal my testimony (for God & humanity) with my blood, will do vastly more toward advancing the cause I have Earnestly endeavored to promote, than all I have done in my life before. I beg of you all meekly and quietly to submit to this; not feeling yourselves to be in the least *degraded* on that account … May God Almighty comfort all your hearts, and soon wipe away all tears from your eyes … "Finally my beloved be of good comfort." May all your names be "written in the Lambs book of life"—May you all have the purifying and sustaining influence of the Christian religion—is the Earnest prayer of your affectionate husband and Father.

John Brown

P.S. I cannot remember a night so dark as to have hindered the coming day: nor a storm so furious or dreadful as to prevent the return of warm sunshine and a cloudless sky. But beloved ones *do remember* that this is not your rest; that in this world you have no abiding place or continuing city. To God and his infinite mercy I always commend you.

Ever Yours

J. B.

In the end, however, Brown said that Mary could visit. She spent an hour talking with him in his cell on December 1. The next day, Brown was led under heavy military guard to an outdoor **scaffold**. The executioner placed a hood over Brown's head, arranged the noose around Brown's neck, and then opened the trapdoor beneath the condemned man. Brown dropped through, and the noose broke his neck.

JOHN BROWN ASCENDING THE SCAFFOLD PREPARATORY TO BEING HANGED.—FROM A SKETCH BY OUR SPECIAL ARTIST.

Brown climbs to the scaffold where he will be hanged. His final words were a note slipped to his jailer.

Before leaving the jail, Brown had handed his jailer a note. It read: "I John Brown am now quite *certain* that the crimes of this *guilty* land will *never* be purged *away* but with Blood. I had *as I now think*, vainly flattered myself that without *very much* bloodshed it might be done." Brown was right about one thing. The crime of slavery would be removed from the land during the great bloodletting of the Civil War, fifteen months away.

CHAPTER FOUR

"His Soul Is Marching On"

John Brown had declared that he wanted to be buried on his North Elba farm, and he was. The authorities sent his body home from Virginia, and Mary Brown held his funeral on the farm on December 8. She added her husband's name to his grandfather's tombstone and placed it over the grave.

Brown was dead, but the uproar he had caused did not soon die down—in the North or in the South.

The "New Saint"

Abolitionists, many of whom had draped their houses and businesses with black cloth on the day of Brown's execution, were loud in their praise of the martyr.

Brown was buried on his farm in North Elba, New York, under the gravestone that had marked his grandfather's burial place.

Harriet Tubman, a leader in the Underground Railroad, spoke of "how he gave up his life for our people."

Ralph Waldo Emerson, a Massachusetts writer, was one of many who used terms from religion when he called Brown "a new saint."

Publisher William Lloyd Garrison also viewed Brown through the lens of religious

Harriet Tubman was one of many who praised Brown's fight against slavery.

belief. On December 16, two weeks after Brown's death, Garrison delivered a thundering speech to a packed crowd. It included these lines:

> I not only desire, but have labored unremittingly to effect the peaceful abolition of slavery, by an appeal to the reason and conscience of the slaveholder; yet, as a peace man—an "ultra" peace man—I am prepared to say, "Success to every slave insurrection at the South, and in every slave country." And I do not see how I compromise or stain my peace profession in making that declaration. Whenever there is a contest between the oppressed and the oppressor,—the weapons being equal between the parties,—God knows that my heart must be with the oppressed, and always against the oppressor. Therefore, whenever commenced, I cannot but wish success to all slave insurrections. … Rather than see men wearing their chains in a cowardly and servile spirit,

Abolitionist William Lloyd Garrison used patriotism and religion to justify Brown's deeds.

Garrison's paper, *The Liberator,* was a leading voice of abolitionism.
This November 1859 issue appeared a few weeks before Brown's death.

I would, as an advocate of peace, much rather
see them breaking the head of the tyrant
with their chains … We have been warmly
sympathizing with John Brown all the way
through, from the time of his arrest till now.
Now he no longer needs our sympathy, for
he is beyond suffering, and wears the victor's
crown … I see in every slave on the Southern
plantation a living John Brown … I see four
millions of living John Browns needing our
thoughts, our sympathies, our prayers, our
noblest exertions to strike off their fetters …

"His Soul Is Marching On"   43

Who instigated John Brown? Let us see. It must have been Patrick Henry, who said–and he was a Virginian– "Give me liberty, or give me death!" … It must have been Thomas Jefferson—another Virginian—who said of the bondage of the Virginia slaves, that "one hour of it is fraught with more misery than ages of that which our fathers rose in rebellion to oppose"—and who, as the author of the Declaration of Independence, proclaimed it to be "a SELF-EVIDENT TRUTH, that all men are created equal, and endowed by their Creator with AN INALIENABLE RIGHT TO LIBERTY" … We have a natural right, therefore, to seek the abolition of slavery throughout the globe … God commands us to "hide the outcasts, and bewray not him that wandereth." I say, LET THE WILL OF GOD BE DONE!

Garrison knew that his speech would be printed in many newspapers. He crafted it to make several key points. One point is that Garrison himself was a peaceful man, not someone who would perform acts of violence. (Many abolitionists hurried to make this point after the raid on Harpers Ferry.) At the same time, Garrison supported and even encouraged slave insurrections, even violent ones, because they were the actions of oppressed slaves against tyrant masters—although this skirts the fact that Brown's raid was not a slave rebellion.

Finally, Garrison touched on two points that, for him and many abolitionists, demanded action against slavery: patriotism and religion. Garrison mentioned Patrick Henry and Thomas Jefferson, heroes of the Revolutionary era, and quoted from the Declaration of Independence. He then quoted from the Bible: God's commandment to the faithful to hide outcasts and not bewray (an old form of "betray") them is from Isaiah 16:3. Garrison framed Brown's actions as a sacred duty to both the nation and God.

Not all abolitionists agreed with Brown's methods, however, and not all Northerners were abolitionists. Some Northerners gathered at meetings and rallies to hear speakers condemn Brown and his "invasion of Virginia," as a religious paper in New York called it. Four days after Brown's execution, the *New York Journal of Commerce* predicted that the "infamous" raid on Harpers Ferry would bring about "a coming together from all places and parties" and unite Americans in support of the Constitution and law.

Reaction in the South

While African Americans and white abolitionists in the North honored Brown with "Martyr's Day" and put his picture in places of honor in their homes, Southerners seethed with fear and anger.

The raid on Harpers Ferry had filled the South with fresh fears of slave uprisings. A string of barn fires in Virginia was blamed on slaves. Rumors spread that abolitionists, or slaves, or both were planning to poison

John Brown's Body

In April 1861, some Union soldiers were marching near Boston. To the tune of an old hymn titled "Say, Brothers, Will You Meet Us," they began teasing a soldier who happened to be named John Brown, singing: "This can't be John Brown … poor old John Brown is dead."

As the song spread, the words changed until the song was about the abolitionist. "John Brown's Body," as it came to be known, included these lines:

> John Brown's body lies a-moldering in the grave,
>
> His soul is marching on …
>
> He captured Harpers Ferry with his nineteen men so true,
>
> He frightened old Virginia 'til she trembled through and through,
>
> They hung him for a traitor, themselves the traitor crew,
>
> His soul is marching on.

In 1862, a different version was published under the title "Battle Hymn of the Republic." The music was the same, but new lyrics had been penned by Julia Ward Howe, the wife of one of Brown's Secret Six backers. The "Battle Hymn" describes God's justice being worked upon the sinful South. After the Civil War, the song remained popular as a religious hymn and patriotic anthem.

John Brown and the Armed Resistance to Slavery

wells, set fire to slaveholders' homes, and slaughter whites. Any abolitionist who ventured into the South—or any innocent traveler who happened to carry a Northern newspaper—risked a beating.

To prevent the insurrection they feared, some Southern communities and states ignored the law or passed new antiblack laws. Armed whites raided slave quarters and also the homes of free black people, searching for weapons. Blacks suspected of planning rebellions were hanged with no trial. Some states required free blacks to either leave the state or offer themselves as slaves.

Southerners were enraged by what they saw as Northern approval of Brown's actions. To them, Brown's raid was a sign that the law meant nothing and that Northern abolitionists meant to destroy the South by any means necessary. On the floor of the US Senate, a Mississippi senator named Albert Gallatin said to Northern senators: "[D]isguise it as you will, there is throughout all the nonslaveholding States of this Union a secret, deep-rooted sympathy with the object which [Brown] had in view." Gallatin accused the entire North of supporting a violent attack on the slaveholding South.

Edmund Ruffin of Virginia belonged to a group of proslavery activists known as the Fire-Eaters, who thought that the South should **secede** from, or leave, the United States. Ruffin wrote in his journal that the raid on Harpers Ferry was just what was "needed to stir the sluggish blood of the South." He joined the cadet corps of the Virginia Military Institute so that he could attend Brown's execution. He managed to get hold of some

Southerner Edmund Ruffin was present at Brown's execution and at the start of the Civil War. He shot himself after the South surrendered.

of the iron pikes that Brown had had made to arm the slaves, and he sent them to Southern governors, warning that "our Northern brethren" meant to kill Southerners. Less than two years later, Ruffin was present when Southern forces fired upon federal troops in Fort Sumter, South Carolina—the military action that started the Civil War. In 1865, after the South surrendered to the North, ending the war, Ruffin shot himself to death.

Also at Brown's execution was a young actor named John Wilkes Booth, who had borrowed a military uniform to mingle with the guard. Six years later, Booth would commit his own dramatic political act: the **assassination** of President Abraham Lincoln, whom he called a tyrant for fighting against the **secession** of the South. Like Brown, Booth claimed to be carrying out divine will. He wrote in his diary: "Our country owed all her troubles to [Lincoln], and God simply made me the instrument of his punishment."

Legend and Legacy

Stories began to be told about John Brown almost at once. According to one early story, as Brown walked to the scaffold to be hanged, an African-American woman pushed through the crowd and held her child up for Brown to kiss. Northern newspapers reported this encounter, and John Greenleaf Whittier, an abolitionist and poet, described it in "John Brown of Osawatomie," published three weeks after Brown's execution:

> John Brown of Osawatomie, they led him out to die;
>
> And lo! a poor slave-mother with her little child pressed nigh.
>
> Then the bold, blue eye grew tender, and the old, harsh face grew mild.
>
> As he stooped between the jeering ranks and kissed the negro's child!

The poem may show how Whittier felt about Brown, but it is not a reliable source of information. Historians do not know how the kiss story started, but they know

The story of Brown kissing a black child on the way to the scaffold was not true, but it was irresistible to poets and artists.

that it is **apocryphal,** or not true. Brown was under heavy military guard at his execution; no member of the public got close to him. The story is an example of how the line between fiction and fact can become blurry over time, as apocryphal stories are repeated. Supporters of Brown may have spread the story because it showed him as a gentle, loving person.

Whittier was not the only poet to write about Brown. In 1921, the American poet Edward Arlington Robinson published a book of poetry that included "John Brown," a poem in the voice of Brown, speaking to his wife before his death. The book received a literary honor called the Pulitzer Prize for poetry. Eight years later another American writer, Stephen Vincent Benét, published a book-length poem about the Civil War titled *John Brown's Body*. It also won the Pulitzer Prize.

Novelists have written about Brown, too. In Russell Banks's *Cloudsplitter* (1994), Brown's son Owen tells

Raymond Massey (lower left, with beard) played the part of John Brown in the 1940 film *Santa Fe Trail*.

the story of his father's life. James McBride's *The Good Lord Bird* (2013), which won the National Book Award for fiction, is narrated by a young slave with Brown at Harpers Ferry. Yet not all portrayals of Brown in fiction are sympathetic. In the 1940 movie *The Santa Fe Trail*, Brown is a dangerous fanatic who was leading the nation to war.

Brown remains a fascinating, complex, and sometimes troubling subject for historians, activists, and anyone interested in American slavery and the Civil War. A stream of scholarly books about Brown has been published since his death, and new ones continue to appear. Depending on the author's point of view, Brown was a hero, was mentally ill, was responsible for abolition and the civil rights movement, or started the bloodiest war in American history. The most common image

American terrorist Timothy McVeigh used a car bomb to attack this federal building in Oklahoma City in 1995. He claimed Brown as an inspiration.

of Brown today is of a man of strong religious faith and moral principles who was driven to violence and bloodshed by the evils of slavery.

A few modern terrorists have said that Brown inspired them. One was a minister who murdered a doctor in Florida in 1994. Another was Timothy McVeigh, who set off an explosion in Oklahoma City in 1995, killing 168 innocent people, including children. Brown chose violence because he believed his cause was right and his goal could not be reached any other way—but every terrorist would say the same.

In John Brown's time, people both opposed and defended slavery, just as they both condemned and praised Brown's actions. Today no one would defend slavery, but the debate over Brown's actions continues. Perhaps John Brown's lasting legacy is that he gives each generation an opportunity to study his story and ask challenging questions.

Chronology

Dates in green pertain to events discussed in this volume.

1619 The African slave trade begins in North America.

1789 US Constitution goes into effect.

1777–1804 Slavery is abolished in the Northern states.

1800 John Brown is born May 9 in Torrington, Connecticut.

1805 Brown family moves to Ohio.

1808 The foreign slave trade is abolished by Great Britain and the United States.

1820 John Brown marries Dianthe Lusk.

1831 Garrison starts publishing *The Liberator* in Boston.

1833 American Anti-Slavery Society is founded in Philadelphia; a year after his first wife dies, John Brown marries Mary Ann Day.

1837 Abolitionist Elijah Lovejoy is killed by a proslavery mob; Brown dedicates himself to the cause of abolishing slavery.

1837–1839 The Grimké sisters speak against slavery to overflow audiences in New York and New England.

1845 *Narrative of the Life of Frederick Douglass* is published.

1846 Brown moves to Springfield, Massachusetts, a center of the abolitionist movement.

1847 Brown discusses abolition with Frederick Douglass.

1849 Harriet Tubman escapes from slavery into Pennsylvania.

1850 US Congress passes the Fugitive Slave Act; Brown organizes a militant group called the League of Gileadites to protect escaped slaves.

1851 *Uncle Tom's Cabin* runs as a serial in the abolitionist newspaper *National Era* in Washington, DC.

1852 Douglass gives famous "Fourth of July" speech in Rochester; Stowe's complete novel, *Uncle Tom's Cabin*, sells millions of copies.

1854 Congress approves the Kansas-Nebraska Act.

1855 Brown goes to Kansas, a battleground for proslavery and antislavery forces.

1855–1860 Harriet Tubman rescues freedom seekers and leads them from Maryland to Canada.

1856 Proslavery activists attack the antislavery town of Lawrence, Kansas; John Brown leads a raid on a proslavery family, which launches a three-month conflict known as "Bleeding Kansas."

1857 The Supreme Court rules on the Dred Scott case.

1858 Brown organizes a constitutional convention in Canada, with the goal of raising support for the freeing of American slaves; later he spends six months in Kansas.

1859 In July, Brown rents a farmhouse near Harpers Ferry; on October 16, he and his men launch their raid on Harpers Ferry, with the goal of capturing the weapons in the arsenal; on October 17, the raiders are surrounded; on October 18, Brown and the surviving raiders are captured by federal troops; found guilty of treason, Brown is hanged on December 2.

1860 Abraham Lincoln is elected president; South Carolina secedes from the Union.

1861 Civil War begins.

1863 Lincoln's Emancipation Proclamation frees the slaves in Confederate-held territory.

1865 The Civil War ends. President Lincoln is assassinated. The Thirteenth Amendment to the US Constitution abolishes slavery.

1866 The American Equal Rights Association is formed.

Its goals are to establish equal rights and the vote for women and African Americans.

1868 Fourteenth Amendment grants US citizenship to former slaves.

1870 Fifteenth Amendment gives black men the right to vote.

1896 A group of black civil rights activists form the National Association of Colored Women in Washington, DC. The group works to further civil rights for blacks and obtain the vote for women.

Glossary

abolitionism The movement to end slavery and free enslaved people.

abolitionist A supporter of abolitionism; someone against slavery.

apocryphal Widely believed to be true or authentic, but in fact is not true.

arsenal Storage place for weapons and ammunition.

assassination Murder of a particular individual to achieve a political goal.

asylum A place of refuge, or a facility for the housing and treatment of people with certain medical conditions, such as insanity.

chattel slavery A form of slavery in which the law defines slaves as property and in which they have few, or no, legal rights.

conspiracy A group of two or more people planning to commit an illegal act.

federal Having to do with the national, or central, government as opposed to state or local government.

incite To urge, inspire, or encourage others to do something.

insurrection A rebellion or uprising.

martyr Someone who willingly dies for a cause and whose death may inspire others.

moral Having to do with questions of right and wrong behavior; a moral person is one whose behavior is right, or good.

orator Someone who makes a speech.

Puritan Having to do with a branch of Protestant Christianity that developed in England and North America in the sixteenth and seventeenth centuries; Puritans believed that people, families, and communities should follow God's will in all things and that they were meant to do God's work on Earth.

satire The use of humor, fantasy, or exaggeration to criticize or make a point about human behavior and weaknesses, or about politics or public affairs.

scaffold A platform raised above the ground on which executions by hanging are carried out; the person to be hanged stands on a trapdoor built in the platform, and when the trapdoor opens the person drops and is killed by the noose around his or her neck.

Glossary

secede To leave a union made up of multiple parts; in nineteenth-century America, some in the South wanted to secede from the Union, or the United States.

secession The act or result of seceding.

slavery A system in which some people's rights and freedoms are controlled by others, who dictate what the enslaved people must do.

terrorist Someone who uses illegal violence or the threat of violence to make a political point or influence a government.

treason An action that is deliberately intended to overthrow or harm one's own government.

Further Information

Books

Cox, Clinton. *Fiery Vision: The Life and Death of John Brown*. New York: Scholastic, 1997.

Marrin, Albert. *A Volcano Beneath the Snow: John Brown's War Against Slavery*. New York: Knopf Books for Young Readers, 2014.

McNeese, Tim. *The Abolition Movement: Ending Slavery*. New York: Chelsea House, 2007.

Schraff, Anne E. *John Brown: "We Came To Free the Slaves."* Berkeley Heights, NJ: Enslow, 2010.

Yancey, Diane. *The Abolition of Slavery*. San Diego: ReferencePoint Press, 2012.

Further Information

Websites

"His Soul Goes Marching On": The Life and Legacy of John Brown

www.wvculture.org/history/jbexhibit/jbintroduction.html

The West Virginia Division of Culture and History presents an online exhibit about the life and legacy of John Brown, including photographs and links to many primary sources.

John Brown

www.pbs.org/wgbh/aia/part4/4p1550.html

This PBS page devoted to John Brown and the raid on Harpers Ferry includes links to additional information and several primary sources.

National Abolition Hall of Fame and Museum

www.nationalabolitionhalloffameandmuseum.org/visitor.html

John Brown is just one of the antislavery activists recognized by the National Abolition Hall of Fame and Museum in Peterboro, New York.

Bibliography

Ayers, Edward L., and Carolyn R. Martin, eds. *America on the Eve of the Civil War.* Charlottesville, VA: University of Virginia Press, 2010.

Carton, Evan. *Patriotic Treason: John Brown and the Soul of America.* New York: Free Press, 2006.

Earle, Jonathan. *John Brown's Raid on Harpers Ferry: A Brief History with Documents.* New York: Bedford/ St. Martin's, 2008.

Horwitz, Tony. *Midnight Rising: John Brown and the Raid that Sparked the Civil War.* New York: Henry Holt, 2011.

McGinty, Brian. *John Brown's Trial.* Cambridge, MA: Harvard University Press, 2009.

Reynolds, David. *John Brown, Abolitionist: The Man Who Killed Slavery, Sparked the Civil War, and Seeded Civil Rights.* New York: Vintage, 2006.

Ronda, Bruce A. *Reading the Old Man: John Brown in American Culture.* Knoxville, TN: University of Tennessee Press, 2008.

Sanborn, Franklin Benjamin. *The Life and Letters of John Brown: Liberator of Kansas, and Martyr of Virginia.* Boston: Roberts Brothers, 1885.

Stauffer, John, and Zoe Trodd, eds. *The Tribunal: Responses to John Brown and the Harpers Ferry Raid.* Cambridge, MA: Harvard University Press, 2012.

Index

About the Author

REBECCA STEFOFF grew up in the Midwest, completed graduate studies in English literature at the University of Pennsylvania, and now lives in the Pacific Northwest. She has written books for young readers on many topics in history, literature, science, and exploration. Her books on American history include *Lewis and Clark: Explorers of the American West* (Chelsea House, 1992), *Tecumseh and the Shawnee Confederation* (Facts On File, 1998), *Surviving the Oregon Trail* (Enslow, 2012), and five volumes in Marshall Cavendish's American Voices series, which focused on primary sources. Recent publications include the six-volume series Is It Science? (Cavendish Square, 2014) and the four-volume series Animal Behavior Revealed (Cavendish Square, 2014). You can learn more about Stefoff and her books for young people at www.rebeccastefoff.com.